Pablo

By United Library

https://campsite.bio/unitedlibrary

Table of Contents

Disclaimer

This biography book is a work of nonfiction based on the public life of a famous person. The author has used publicly available information to create this work. While the author has thoroughly researched the subject and attempted to depict it accurately, it is not meant to be an exhaustive study of the subject. The views expressed in this book are those of the author alone and do not necessarily reflect those of any organization associated with the subject. This book should not be taken as an endorsement, legal advice, or any other form of professional advice. This book was written for entertainment purposes only.

Introducción

Immerse yourself in the fascinating story of Pablo Emilio Escobar Gaviria, Colombia's infamous drug trafficker, as this book unveils the life of a man who rose from humble beginnings to become the kingpin of the notorious Medellin Cartel. Born into a rural family, Escobar showed early business skills, embarking on a criminal journey in the late 1960s through smuggling and then venturing into the production and distribution of marijuana and cocaine globally in the late 1970s.

Forming key alliances with the likes of Gonzalo Rodríguez Gacha, Carlos Lehder and Jorge Luis Ochoa, Escobar established the Medellín Cartel, achieving unprecedented domination of the cocaine trade, controlling over 80% of global production and 60% of the illicit market in the United States. His criminal empire amassed a staggering $8 billion in wealth, cementing his status as one of the world's richest individuals for seven consecutive years.

While attempting to improve his image through charity events and a brief foray into politics, Escobar faced public accusations of illegal activities, resulting in the loss of his congressional seat in 1983. The 1980s saw the height of narcoterrorism as Escobar declared war on the Colombian government, orchestrating violent acts, assassinations and bombings that rocked the nation.

Amid a backdrop of intense conflict, including battles with rival cartels and paramilitary groups, Escobar's escape from La Catedral, a prison he engineered, marked a turning point. The government's relentless pursuit culminated in a shootout on a Medellín rooftop in 1993, ending the life of one of history's most notorious criminals.

This book navigates the complexities of Escobar's criminal empire, his strategic maneuvers and the devastating impact of his reign, offering readers a captivating account of the power, violence and ultimate downfall of the man who became the world's most wanted fugitive.

Pablo Escobar

Pablo Emilio Escobar Gaviria (Rionegro, Antioquia; December 1, 1949 - Medellín; December 2, 1993) was a Colombian drug trafficker, criminal, terrorist and politician, founder and top leader of the Medellín Cartel.

Born into a peasant family, Escobar would demonstrate a knack for business from an early age; he began his criminal life in the late 1960s in smuggling, and in the late 1970s became involved in the production and marketing of marijuana and cocaine abroad.

After forming alliances with Gonzalo Rodríguez Gacha, Carlos Lehder and Jorge Luis Ochoa and their clan, Escobar founded the Medellín Cartel, an organization that at its peak monopolized the cocaine business from production to consumption, controlling more than 80% of the world's cocaine production and 60% of the illicit cocaine market in the United States.He managed to consolidate his criminal empire, making him the most powerful man in the Colombian mafia, accumulating an immense fortune of around 8 billion dollars in assets and cash, making him one of the richest men in the world according to *Forbes magazine* for seven consecutive years.

To excuse his immense capital, in the early 1980s Escobar tried to polish his image through charity work for the underprivileged and a brief incursion into politics, occupying a seat as a representative to the Chamber of Deputies in the National Congress in 1982. However, in 1983, after several publications in the newspaper *El Espectador* and with the direct accusation of the Minister of Justice Rodrigo Lara Bonilla, he lost his seat and was publicly accused of his illegal business. Some time later, Rodrigo Lara Bonilla in 1984 and Guillermo Cano, director of *El Espectador,* were assassinated by orders of Escobar.

By 1985, drug trafficking was booming and cartels were dominating Colombia, sparking a war against the government, headed at the time by Belisario Betancur. The latter was the one who had appointed Rodrigo Lara Bonilla as Minister of Justice, who had pointed out drug traffickers who were involved in politics, economy, and even in the world of soccer.

The narcos had private armies, businesses throughout Colombia, large tracts of land and control of markets such as emeralds. Later, Lara dismantled the Medellín Cartel's largest cocaine laboratory, *Tranquilandia*, and seized 30 of the same group's airplanes. The narcos' war against the government became violent and sadistic.

After several negotiation attempts and multiple kidnappings and selective assassinations of judges and public officials, in 1989, the Medellín Cartel, with Escobar at the helm, declared total war against the State.He organized and financed an extensive network of hitmen, loyal to his command, who assassinated key personalities for the Colombian institutionality, such as the liberal leader Luis Carlos Galán, and perpetrated indiscriminate terrorist acts with the use of car bombs in the main cities of the country that destabilized it, and brought the authorities "to their knees", and made him the most wanted criminal in the world in the early 1990s.He was responsible for the murder of 657 policemen between 1989 and 1993, and for fierce confrontations against the Cali Cartel, the Magdalena Medio paramilitaries and finally *Los Pepes*.

After the consummation of the National Constituent Assembly in 1991, which gave Colombia a new constitution and prohibited the extradition of nationals to the United States, Escobar decided to submit to justice on the sole condition that he be held in *La Catedral*, an ostentatious prison located on his land. After it was shown that he was still committing crimes behind bars, the government wanted to capture him, so Escobar escaped, easily getting out through the back of the prison, which was one of the most shameful episodes for the country's penitentiary authority. After his escape, the government formed the so-called Search Bloc to recapture him and after 17 months of intense tracking, he was shot on a rooftop in a middle-class sector of Medellín at the age of 44 on December 2, 1993.

Biography

Family

Pablo Emilio Escobar Gaviria was born on December 1, 1949 in the village of *El Tablazo*, located in the rural area of Rionegro, Antioquia, Colombia. His parents were Abel de Jesús Escobar Echeverri (March 14, 1914 - October 25, 2001), a farmer who left an immense fortune when he died, and Hermilda de los Dolores Gaviria Berrío (April 5, 1917 - October 26, 2006), a school teacher.His siblings, in order of birth were: Roberto de Jesús, alias *El Osito*, Gloria Inés, Argemiro, Alba Marina, Luz María and Luis Fernando (the youngest, born in 1958 and murdered at the age of 19 in 1977).

His maternal grandfather, Roberto Gaviria Cobaleda (January 31, 1873 - March 10, 1943), had already preceded him in illegal activities, as he was a renowned Whisky smuggler in times when Whisky was illegal (early 20th century). The aforementioned Roberto Gaviria was also the grandfather of Colombian lawyer and politician José Obdulio Gaviria. José Obdulio has had to fight against his surname. For the last 20 years he has had to cope with the circumstances of being Pablo Escobar Gaviria's cousin.

In an interview given to national television at the time (1980s), Pablo Escobar stated the following about his origins.

However, his ancestors and immediate family members stood out as politicians, businessmen, cattle ranchers and figures of the Antioquian elite, so his much-publicized "popular origins" do not correspond to reality. Among his extensive kinship we can mention Isabel Gaviria Duque, first lady of the Nation, wife of Carlos E. Restrepo, who was president of Colombia between 1910 and 1914. Pablo Escobar's godfather was the renowned Colombian diplomat and intellectual Joaquín Vallejo Arbeláez. In the parish of Rionegro rests his baptismal certificate that reads:

Children and youth

According to his mother's testimony, Escobar began to show insight and astuteness already in elementary school; and in the beginning of high school, another of his qualities became evident, his leadership over his classmates. Escobar and his cousin Gustavo Gaviria Rivero did little "business" at the Lucrecio Jaramillo Vélez high school, where they both studied. They held raffles, traded comic books, sold exams and lent money at low interest rates. In this way, Pablo Escobar began to develop his "skill" for business and commerce.

In 1969 he finished high school at the aforementioned Liceo, then he was admitted to study at the Faculty of Economics at the Universidad Autónoma Latinoamericana in Medellín, where several of his cousins Gaviria, among them José Obdulio, were studying, but finally he chose to withdraw because he preferred to dedicate himself to his personal "business". As a curious fact, he always felt self-conscious about his short stature (1.65) and this made him wear special shoes with heels in order to look taller.

Marriage and children

His wife was Victoria Eugenia Henao Vallejo, *La Tata*, whom he married when she was 15 years old in 1976, and to whom he gave birth to his only two children: Juan Pablo Escobar Henao on February 24, 1977 and Manuela Escobar Henao on May 24, 1984. Gloria Gaviria Flores, who was her spoiled cousin, was the godmother of the wedding along with Carlos Fersch, the best friend of the Southern Cartel. She states that:

Gloria currently lives in Bogota and pays house arrest, the parental authority of her youngest son is held by his grandmother, the last thing that was known about the young man is that he lives in Antioquia, with his grandmother. Escobar's children, Juan Pablo and Manuela Escobar Henao, left their country after Escobar's death, but were returned upon their arrival in the United States and suffered the same fate in Germany. They finally settled in Buenos Aires, Argentina, where they had several legal problems that they later managed to resolve. For security reasons, and to avoid the stigma of having Escobar's last name, their names and surnames were changed by the Colombian authorities before they left that country. Thus, Victoria was renamed María Isabel Santos Caballero, Juan Pablo is now Juan Sebastián Marroquín Santos and Manuela is called Juana Manuela Marroquín Santos, identities that were recently revealed of their own free will.

In 2009, a young man born in San José, Costa Rica, claimed to the press in Colombia to be the son of a relationship that Pablo Escobar allegedly had with a Costa Rican woman in 1974. According to his version, he was raised by his mother in the neighborhood of Desamparados. In 1985, when the boy was 10 years old, his mother took him to the U.S. He called himself Pablo Escobar Jr. and devoted himself to hip hop singing and acting: he was part of the cast of the series *El Cartel de los Sapos* and the soap opera *El rostro de Analía*. Escobar's family denounced that he was an impostor.

On December 11, 2009, his son Juan Pablo presented the biographical documentary *Pecados de mi padre*, in which he asks for forgiveness from families victimized by drug violence.

On November 8, 2006, one day after the death of his mother Hermilda, Escobar's body was exhumed by order of Nicolas Escobar, Pablo's nephew and son of Roberto Escobar Gaviria, alias *El Osito*. Juan Pablo Escobar accused his cousin of having sold the images of the exhumation to television (they were broadcast live) and of profiting from the memory of the assassin. The family dispute deepened after it became known that Nicolas kept three teeth and a piece of the mustache that remained on the skeleton, although he claims that he kept them to carry out DNA tests that would resolve the paternity claims of two alleged children of the drug trafficker.

Criminal career

Escobar's beginnings in organized crime came slowly but surely, and throughout his criminal career, he used a strange mix of violence, blood, paternalism and philanthropy to achieve his ends.While, on the one hand, he ruthlessly eliminated his competitors, ordered assassinations, encouraged intrigues or conspired against influential figures in politics or government, on the other, he gave sandwiches to beggars, built houses for the poor of Medellín or constructed soccer fields for children in the suburbs, which gave him strong popular support in the city's poorest neighborhoods.

Escobar began his criminal career with petty theft and working for Colombia's smuggling king Alfredo Gomez Lopez *"Don Capone"*. Contrary to popular belief, he did not run a bicycle business or steal tombstones to resell them, as he was deeply religious from a very young age, as was his family. Years later he would build several churches, soccer fields and rebuild the city with the income derived from cocaine trafficking.

As he grew older, he became involved in car theft on the streets of Medellín, and soon moved into marijuana trafficking to the United States. He was also implicated in the kidnapping and murder of industrialist Diego

Echavarría Misas in 1971, and of drug lord Fabio Restrepo in 1975. He first acted as a middleman buying coca paste in Colombia, Bolivia and Peru, and then reselling it to the traffickers in charge of taking it to the United States.

In the 1970s, he became a key player in international cocaine trafficking. In association with Gonzalo Rodríguez Gacha, Carlos Lehder, Jorge Luis Ochoa and his brothers Fabio and Juan David, he founded and led the so-called Medellín Cartel, which took control of runways, routes and laboratories and monopolized the illegal trade from production to consumption. In 1976 he was arrested for drug trafficking, but the process was time-barred and he was released months after his arrest. However, the process was reopened by Judge Mariela Espinosa, who also dismissed the investigation due to threats against his life. Espinosa was murdered in 1989, by order of Escobar.

He would later be ranked as the seventh richest man in the world according to *Forbes magazine,* something his son would deny years later. He owned an exotic and extensive hacienda, called Hacienda Nápoles, which became his center of operations.

Pablo Escobar was among the world's multimillionaires due to his immense fortune invested in buildings, houses, cars and haciendas. In the Hacienda Nápoles he gathered more than 200 species of exotic animals for the region, such as hippopotamuses, giraffes, elephants, zebras and ostriches, all introduced into the country as a result of bribing the customs authorities, which did not prevent the property from being shown on television in a propaganda report. He was fond of luxury cars and, after the attack perpetrated by his enemies in the Cali cartel, more than 40 sports cars were found in the parking lot of the Monaco building in Medellin, where part of his family lived. It is difficult to calculate the totality of his real estate assets such as buildings, offices, farms, commercial premises and houses, but some data speak of more than 500 properties owned by him. He also owned helicopters, motorcycles, boats and several small planes to transport drugs through various regions of the country.

According to DEA documents, the Medellín Cartel founded the group Muerte a Secuestradores (MAS) in 1981 as a response to kidnappings (kidnapping of Martha Nieves Ochoa, attempted kidnapping of Carlos Lehder) and guerrilla actions against them, this group is also related, after the death of Pablo Escobar, to Carlos Castaño and his brother Fidel, known paramilitary commanders.

Political activities

In the late 1970s (or early 1970s) he realized that he had to create a "front" in order to protect his lucrative drug trade. He began to cultivate an image of a respectable man, making contact with politicians, financiers, lawyers, etc. Without knowing for sure his true intentions, Pablo Escobar built many charitable works for the poor, among them 60 soccer fields, or an entire neighborhood called "Medellin without slums" - also called "barrio Pablo Escobar".

He imposed the "silver or lead law", whereby many members of the Colombian government, police and military either accepted the "plata" (money) or were showered with "plomo" (shot dead).

He won the support that would lead him to be elected as alternate to the House of Representatives for the Alternativa Liberal movement, after being expelled by Luis Carlos Galán from the New Liberalism together with Jairo Ortega Ramírez. He was invited in 1982 to the inauguration of Felipe González, the third president of democratic Spain, by the Spanish businessman Enrique Sarasola, who had important businesses in Medellín.

In this way, in his best moment he was able to accumulate great influence in multiple civil, economic, religious and social sectors of Medellín, Antioquia and the country.

But his cover began to crumble in 1983, when Justice Minister Rodrigo Lara Bonilla also led an investigation against Escobar when it was discovered that he was involved with money of dubious origin in politics and national soccer teams, publicly accusing him of being one of the founders of the paramilitary group MAS.

The FBI in 1990 produced a report that Escobar allegedly financed political campaigns in the 1990 congressional elections.

The narco-terrorist war

Rodrigo Lara Bonilla's investigations, together with police colonel Jaime Ramírez Gómez, prove Escobar's involvement in drug trafficking when the kingpin had given the minister an *ultimatum* to prove his accusations or else he would accuse him of slander and defamation. The newspaper *El Espectador* published a series of editorial notes written by its director, Guillermo Cano Isaza, which revealed what was really behind Pablo Escobar. Congress, which at first showed a hesitant attitude, removed his parliamentary immunity, and the way was opened for the authorities to start pursuing him.

Escobar, together with Ortega, attacks the minister by showing a check from drug trafficker Evaristo Porras financing Lara's senatorial campaign, but the minister denies any such link and manages to discredit Escobar by publicly showing a U.S. ABC documentary on the drug lord while Ramirez was leading an operation that dismantled *Tranquilandia*, a giant cocaine processing laboratory complex belonging to the cartel, located near the Yari River in the then Guaviare police station. As a result, Escobar loses his seat, his visa to the United States is cancelled and Escobar publicly resigns from politics.

On April 30, 1984, Lara was assassinated on Escobar's orders, beginning a period that has gone down in history as "narcoterrorism". After this event, President Belisario Betancur, previously opposed to the extradition of Colombians, decided to authorize it, triggering a series of police operations to capture members of the Medellín Cartel. The main leaders of the cartel had to take refuge in Panama and in May 1984, in the midst of the so-called Panama Dialogues with former President Alfonso López Michelsen, they attempted a last attempt at rapprochement with the State. Their failure was due to the fact that the dialogues had been leaked to the press. Months later, they would return clandestinely to the country and total war would be a matter of time.

A year after the assassination of Lara Bonilla, despite the government's announcements to combat them, the drug traffickers of the Medellin Cartel, now renamed *Los Extraditables*, remained unpunished, expanding their criminal apparatus throughout large parts of the country and opening new cocaine trafficking routes through Nicaragua and Cuba. All this in collusion with some sectors of the security forces, bought off with money and terror.

In November 1984 "Los Extraditables" exploded a car bomb in front of the U.S. embassy in Bogotá, killing one person and, in June 1985, ordered the death of Judge

Tulio Manuel Castro Gil, in charge of investigating the crime of Lara Bonilla. Escobar, at war with the guerrilla, after the MAS episode, approached the M-19 through negotiations with Iván Marino Ospina. According to some versions, it is believed that he was aware of the seizure of the Palace of Justice due to the threats of *Los Extraditables* to the magistrates of the courts and for having offered economic support for the operation, which has not been accepted by the ex-militants of the M-19, since the operation, according to them, had political objectives. The operation was authorized by Álvaro Fayad and was carried out between November 6 and 7, 1985, leaving 94 dead and 11 people disappeared during the retaking of the Palace by the Public Forces.

The campaign of terror continued against their enemies in the government and those who supported the extradition treaty, made effective in January 1985 with the sending of the first captured to the United States through the recently appointed Minister of Justice Enrique Parejo González, replacing the murdered Lara, and all those who denounced their business and mafia networks. *The Extraditables* assassinated, in February 1986, in Baton Rouge, Louisiana, the pilot and witness before the American justice Barry Seal; in July, the magistrate Hernando Baquero Borda, rapporteur of the Extradition Treaty in 1980, and the journalist of *El Espectador* Roberto Camacho Prada; and on August 18, already with the new president of Colombia Virgilio Barco Vargas, the captain of the anti-narcotics police Luis Alfredo Macana.

They would also demonstrate their corrupt power when they prevented Jorge Luis Ochoa and Gilberto Rodriguez Orejuela, captured in Spain and both known drug traffickers, from being extradited to the United States and deported to Colombia, where they paid derisory prison sentences. Until that time, the country's main drug exporting groups were generally on good terms with each other, although the authorities' attention was essentially focused on the violent Medellin kingpins, who controlled up to 90% of the lucrative business. And although the Cali bosses opted mainly for corruption and infiltration within the institutions as a means of dealing with the state, in September 1986 they ordered the murder of Diario Occidente journalist Raul Echavarria Barrientos.After Virgilio Barco Vargas ascended to the presidency, in September 1986, motorized assassins killed Judge Gustavo Zuluaga Serna, in charge of investigating the death of two DAS agents who, in 1978, had arrested Escobar for drug possession and trafficking. In October 1986, anti-narcotics police colonel Jaime Ramírez Gómez was killed. On December 17, 1986, Guillermo Cano, director of the newspaper *El Espectador,* was killed. In January 1987, Escobar's assassins perpetrated a terrorist attack in Budapest, Hungary, against Enrique Parejo

González, former Minister of Justice and, at the time, Colombian ambassador to that country.

It is believed that Escobar was the one who provoked Lehder's capture and extradition to the United States on February 4, 1987. Escobar and the rest of the leadership, aware of the danger that the extradition represented to their interests and determined to fight it, reinforced their military and economic apparatus and set about the task of raising substantial resources among all the drug traffickers, even among those who were not part of his group, in order to finance the foreseeable escalation of violence.

Cartel war (1986-1993)

The beginning of the rift between the two cartels is not entirely clear. In 1984, when the group "Los Extraditables," associated with the Medellín Cartel, decided to assassinate Rodrigo Lara Bonilla, a pool of drug lords was formed and contributed large sums of money. The Cali Cartel seems to have disapproved of the plan, and sent a message that the crime would be turned against all of them and that if Lara was killed they would not be counted on. Escobar's ambition to dominate the situation motivated a first purge within the organization, among them Pablo Correa Arroyave, and Hugo Hernan Valencia, all through an exchange of favors with Gilberto Rodriguez. After Hélmer Herrera Buitrago refused to hand over Piña, one of his men, Escobar ordered Piña's kidnapping and his murder at the hands of Negro Pabón, one of his lieutenants. The assassination led to a rift between the two cartels. The capture in November 1987 of Jorge Luis Ochoa in Buga (Valle), was seen as a product of a betrayal by the Cali traffickers.

In the midst of this discussion, on January 13, 1988, 70 k of dynamite exploded in front of the Monaco Building, owned by Pablo Escobar and his family's residence.

No one was killed, even though the building was semi-destroyed. Although the Cali Cartel insisted on denying responsibility for the attack, for Escobar it seems to have been the Florero de Llorente that unleashed the open war between cartels. Not only had they messed with him but also with his family and it is said that his daughter was left with serious hearing damage.

From that moment on, an offensive began against the Cali Cartel's businesses and properties. On February 18, 1988, a branch of the Drogas La Rebaja chain in Medellín was set on fire, followed by nearly 40 dynamite attacks against the drugstore chain and 10 more against the Grupo Radial Colombiano, both belonging to the Rodríguez Orejuela family. 1988 marked the beginning of the espionage and counter-espionage offensives. First Escobar mounted an intelligence operation against the Cali Cartel. The Rodriguez Orejuelas, in turn, hired five retired military officers to set up an espionage service against Escobar. Escobar discovered them and kidnapped them. The Cali cartel then made a peace proposal, to which Escobar put two conditions: Compensation of 5 million dollars for the attack against the Monaco building, and the surrender of Pacho Herrera, Escobar's bitter enemy. Gilberto Rodriguez refused to hand over and the five ex-military men appeared dead a few days later with a placard that read. "Members of the Cali Cartel executed for attempting to attack people in Medellín".

In December 1988, Escobar attempts to kidnap Pacho Herrera in Cali, the operation fails and Herrera becomes Escobar's main target.

1989 offensive and negotiations

The possible extradition of Escobar reactivated the offensive against the state. A few days later, politician and Medellín mayoral candidate Juan Gómez Martínez was saved from a kidnapping attempt claimed by Los Extraditables. And although Ochoa was released with impunity under the right of habeas corpus a month later, the confrontation did not stop. In the first days of January 1987, the government - publicly humiliated - issued extradition orders against the main members of the organization. On January 13, Pacho Herrera had the Monaco Building, where Escobar lived with his family, dynamited. The bloody war of hired assassins between the two cartels intensified. Several bombs exploded in the pharmacies of the Drogas La Rebaja chain, owned by the Rodríguez Orejuela family.

On January 16, 1988, Escobar's hired assassins kidnapped Andres Pastrana -candidate for mayor of Bogota and later President of the Republic- and kept him hidden for several days in a farm near Rionegro. On January 25, 1988 they kidnapped Carlos Mauro Hoyos - Attorney General of the Nation (Chief Prosecutor) - as he was on his way to the airport in Rionegro (Antioquia).

That same day, the Rionegro police freed Pastrana, and in retaliation *Popeye* shot dead Carlos Mauro Hoyos (48), who had been kidnapped for 10 hours and whose previous plan was to keep Pastrana and Hoyos kidnapped in the same place. In March 1988, several hundred uniformed men descended on the El Bizcocho farm, owned by Escobar, but he was alerted at the last minute and escaped.

Beginning in July 1988, the Secretary General of the Presidency, German Montoya, had entered into talks with the leaders of Los Extraditables. Subsequent declarations by the government were interpreted by the drug traffickers as an invitation to dialogue, so on September 15, they responded with a letter to the Barco administration and sent Montoya a pardon bill and a demobilization plan. However, given the intransigence of the United States, reluctant to talk with the drug traffickers, the talks were delayed and in the end they were presented as a personal initiative of the intermediary, thus disassociating the president from them.

As a reaction to this dialogue without results, the cartel headed by Escobar and Rodríguez Gacha began a chain of assassinations of judges, government officials and public figures. In March 1989, Los Extraditables killed Héctor Giraldo Gálvez, who had taken over the Lara case from

Castro Gil, and two months later they dynamited the headquarters of the Mundo Visión television station. On May 4, 1989, the former governor of Boyacá Álvaro González Santana, father of Judge Martha Lucía González, was assassinated. After the assassination attempt against the head of the DAS, General Miguel Maza Márquez on May 30, 1989 in Bogotá, using a powerful explosive charge that killed 7, terrorism took over the country. On July 4, 1989, in Medellín, in an attack directed at Colonel Valdemar Franklin Quintero, the governor of Antioquia, Antonio Roldán Betancur, was killed along with five of his companions. On July 28, 1989, Escobar's hired assassins killed Judge María Helena Díaz - Espinoza's substitute - and her two escorts.

On August 16, 1989, Escobar's hired assassins killed the judge of the Superior Court of Cundinamarca, Carlos Ernesto Valencia, and on August 18, in Medellín, Colonel Quintero, who was treacherously riddled with dozens of bullet wounds. Although the news of the crime occurred in the morning hours was overshadowed, when at night during a political rally in Soacha, several dozens of gunmen at the service of Rodríguez Gacha infiltrated the demonstration and killed the presidential pre-candidate for the liberal party, Luis Carlos Galán, a staunch enemy of drug traffickers and supporter of allowing the extradition of drug traffickers to the United States, who had the best chances of winning the presidency of the nation. The assassination also involved the politician Alberto Santofimio Botero, who in 2006 was shown to have been an intellectual co-author of the crime.

As a consequence of Galán's assassination, the dialogues were completely interrupted and the president declared war on drug trafficking in the same way that Betancur had done five years earlier. With Decree 1830 of August 19, 1989, Barco established extradition through administrative channels, without the Supreme Court's ruling; with Decree 1863 he authorized military judges to carry out searches where there was presumption or evidence of persons or objects related to a crime; With Decree 1856 it ordered the confiscation of all movable and immovable property of drug traffickers; and with Decree 1859 it authorized the detention in conditions of absolute incommunicado detention and for a period of time that exceeded constitutional norms, of persons of whom there were serious indications of having committed crimes against the existence and security of the State. In addition, the creation of the Elite Group with 500 men was ordered, essentially aimed at hunting down terrorist ringleaders and placed under the command of Colonel Hugo Martínez Poveda. In the following days, the Army and the Police carried out more than 450 raids throughout the national territory and arrested nearly 13,000 people accused of being linked to drug trafficking.

On August 23, Los Extraditables responded to the government in a letter to the public, taking on the challenge of total war. With 3,000 armed assassins, the association of paramilitarism and the support of a significant portion of the population under its control, in addition to the financial muscle that gave it control of at least 90% of the cocaine trafficking abroad, the Medellin Cartel confronted the Colombian State with bombings and selective assassinations. Between September and December 1989, more than 100 devices exploded in Bogotá, Medellín, Cali, Bucaramanga, Cartagena, Barranquilla and Pereira, targeting government buildings, banking, commercial and service facilities and economic infrastructure. In those three months, adding up the hired assassination attacks, the narco-terrorists were responsible for 289 terrorist attacks in that period, with a fatal toll of 300 civilians killed and more than 1,500 wounded.

On August 30, 1989, the first bomb exploded in Medellín; on September 2, the facilities of the newspaper *El Espectador* were almost destroyed; on September 11, Escobar's hitmen assassinated the liberal leader Pablo Peláez González; on September 21, Escobar's hitmen dynamited 9 political offices in Teusaquillo; and on September 26, they attacked the Hilton Hotel in Cartagena. Despite not being able to stop the continuous explosions, the authorities did not let up in their efforts, they multiplied the raids and captured two major capos: Eduardo Martinez Romero and Rafael *El Mono* Abello, to later extradite them to the United States. In retaliation, on October 16, 1989, a car bomb destroyed the headquarters of the *Vanguardia Liberal* newspaper (Bucaramanga) and killed 4 journalists. On November 8, 1989, Escobar's hired assassins killed Judge Héctor Jiménez Rodríguez and journalist Jorge Enrique Pulido (who had already received threats) when he was about to return to his program after the Sunday broadcast of the *Mundo Visión* news program, receiving several bullet wounds. Luis Francisco Madero (Representative to the Chamber of Deputies) was also killed. At the end of October, seven policemen were killed in Medellín, five of them in the explosion of a bus in front of the Officers' Club in the city.

On November 23, 1989, a lightning operation was launched against the El Oro hacienda in Cocorná (Antioquia) where Pablo Escobar and Jorge Luis Ochoa were staying. Escobar managed to escape, but two of his men were killed - one of them his brother-in-law, Fabio Henao - and 55 were arrested. Four days later, on November 27, Escobar's assassins blew up Avianca flight 203 in order to kill the then candidate César Gaviria Trujillo, Galán's successor (who had not boarded the plane on the advice of his advisors), resulting in 107 civilians killed. On December 6, 1989, Escobar's assassins placed a bus bomb in front of the building of the DAS -the Colombian secret police-, trying to assassinate its director, General Miguel Alfredo Maza Márquez, who escaped unharmed despite the fact that the building was semi-destroyed. The bus-bomb also destroyed more than 200 commercial establishments around it. Sixty-three civilians were killed and 500 wounded.

On December 15, 1989, the Barco government succeeded in killing the second leader of the Medellín cartel and its military leader, *El Mexicano* (Rodríguez Gacha). He was located by an informant on the northern coast of the country, where he was taking refuge from persecution by the authorities. Responsible for more than 2000 homicides and claiming responsibility for the attack on the DAS building, he was killed after a hard chase between the municipalities of Tolú and Coveñas in the department of Sucre, together with his son Freddy Rodríguez Celades, his main lieutenant Gilberto Rendón Hurtado and four hitmen from his security corps. Most of the terrorist attacks in recent months were attributed to the Mexican. The Extraditables tried a new strategy of dialogue and negotiation with the State, trying to pressure it with the kidnapping of the son of the Secretary of the Presidency, Alvaro Diego Montoya and two relatives of the President of the Republic. A proposal was made by former president López Michelsen, supported by former presidents Julio César Turbay and Misael Pastrana,

Cardinal Mario Rebollo Bravo and UP president Diego Montaña Cuellar, to form a commission of Notables to negotiate with the narcoterrorists.

On January 17, 1990, they responded to this proposal by presenting themselves in a communiqué as legitimate aspirants to judicial pardon and expressed a "true willingness to negotiate". Immediately afterwards they freed the hostages, handed over a bus with a ton of dynamite and one of the largest drug processing laboratories in Chocó. In return, the drug traffickers expected the government to create a high-level commission that would be in charge of the legal procedures that would allow them to surrender. However, this never happened and the attempt at dialogue and negotiation ended in a new wave of terrorism.

Effectively deceived by the government and faced with a strong military offensive in Envigado, declared a military operations zone by the IV Brigade under the command of General Harold Bedoya, the extraditables put an end to the truce on March 30, putting a price on the head of each dead policeman. Medellín and its metropolitan area became embroiled in a real urban war, after the first executions of uniformed officers and after the attack on a truck belonging to the Elite Group, which occurred on a bridge in Itagüí on April 11. This attack, which left 20 dead and 100 wounded, was the first of 18 that followed until the end of July, resulting in 100 fatalities and 450 wounded.

On May 12, the eve of Mother's Day celebrations, bombs exploded in two commercial neighborhoods of Bogota, killing 21 people. On the same day in Cali another terrorist act took the lives of 9 civilians. At the end of the month, while a hitman blew himself up in front of the Intercontinental Hotel in Medellín, killing 6 policemen and 3 bystanders, Senator Federico Estrada Vélez and his driver were gunned down. Violence intensified and the victims were thousands: in retaliation for the death of 215 uniformed men executed between April and July 1990, death squads went up every night to the communes and shot dozens of men, several of them minors.

Shortly after Escobar's military chief, *Pinina* (John Jairo Arias Tascón), was assassinated on June 14, another series of warlike actions followed: 19 young men from Antioquian high society were killed in the Oporto Bar Massacre and a car bomb exploded in front of the Libertadores Police Station, killing 14 civilians. Finally, at the end of July, after an immense operation in the Magdalena Medio Antioqueño from which Escobar escaped once again, Los Extraditables decreed a new truce and went on the defensive, awaiting the decisions that the incoming Gaviria administration could take. In any case, they affirm the impossibility of surrendering to justice as long as the state security agencies are not restructured and the appropriate legal mechanisms are not created to prevent their extradition.

Bombings and kidnappings. Surrender and surrender

Apart from an unfinished peace process, President César Gaviria inherited the "war against drug trafficking" with which his predecessor had intended to reduce the Medellín Cartel and its network of hired assassins, declared enemies of the State. Although during his presidential campaign he had shown full support both for the offensive and for the measures taken by the first president, among them the one most feared by the narco-terrorists, which was extradition through administrative channels, once in office he let it be known that the high economic and human cost of this war deserved the search for an alternative solution in which the strengthening of justice would be a key element. In any case, on August 12, in a coup d'état, men of the Elite Group killed Gustavo Gaviria Rivero, Pablo Escobar's cousin and right-hand man.

Taking advantage of the respite of the indefinite unilateral truce announced in July by Los Extraditables, Justice Minister Jaime Giraldo Angel designed the state of siege legislation that would be made public as a "policy of submission to justice. This policy, which materialized in five decrees that would later be elevated, after a purge, to permanent legislation in the new Code of Criminal Procedure, aimed, in simplified terms, to favor drug traffickers who voluntarily surrendered and confessed to at least one crime, with the guarantee, in some cases conditional, of being tried in the country and held in high-security prisons. The first to accept the offer, between December 1990 and February 1991, were the Ochoa brothers, Jorge Luis, Juan David and Fabio, close associates of Escobar, who, suspicious of the Government's intentions, which had already failed to comply, organized a series of selective kidnappings of well-known journalists and influential national figures.

Escobar ordered the kidnapping of relatives of members of the Government and journalists, of the long list of kidnapped the most recognized were: Francisco Santos Calderón (editor-in-chief of the newspaper *El Tiempo*), Maruja Pachón de Villamizar (journalist and general director of Focine, wife of politician and diplomat Alberto Villamizar), Beatriz Villamizar de Guerrero (sister of Alberto Villamizar and personal assistant of FOCINE), Diana Turbay (director of the television news program Criptón and the magazine Hoy x Hoy, daughter of former President of the Republic Julio César Turbay) and who died in confusing events during a police rescue attempt,

Marina Montoya de Pérez (sister of former Secretary General of the Presidency Germán Montoya) and who died during a police rescue attempt, Germán Montoya) and who is executed by her captors in retaliation for the death of hitmen and collaborators of the cartel at the hands of the police, especially for the death of the brothers Armando and Ricardo Prisco Lopera, leaders of Los Priscos, the armed wing of the cartel, Álvaro Diego Montoya (eldest son of the then secretary general of the Presidency, Germán Montoya), Patricia Echeverri and his daughter Diana Echeverri, in-laws of former President Barco, thus pressuring the outgoing president-elect to be treated as a political criminal, and in the process benefiting from the pardons reserved for guerrillas. Escobar also tried to obtain from the Executive a tailor-made agreement and continued to exert pressure again by armed means, threatening to execute the hostages and to restart his terrorist offensive.

On December 13, 1990, a bomb killed 7 policemen in Medellín and 7 more were killed by hired assassins in the first 3 days of January and with a new spate of attacks: a dozen police officers were victims of hired assassins, an explosion in a bus left 6 dead and on February 16, an atrocious bombing against an F2 patrol car in Medellín in front of the city's bullring, left 22 civilians dead. Two months later, Escobar's assassins killed former Justice Minister Enrique Low Murtra in Bogotá.

The government had to give in to Escobar's demands, who released the rest of the hostages as a gesture of "good faith". But only when he was sure that the National Constituent Assembly had voted and approved on June 19, 1991 the article that prohibited the extradition of Colombians by birth, Escobar surrendered with Father Rafael García Herreros and Alberto Villamizar, mediators in his surrender. He would later be imprisoned in the famous La Catedral Prison in Envigado. From there, despite promises not to commit any more crimes, he continued to control the strings of the illegal business through two other allies of his who did not surrender: Fernando *El Negro* Galeano and Gerardo *Kiko* Moncada and several of his hitmen.

War in the Magdalena Medio

Since the policy of plea bargaining also covered the paramilitaries, many members of the organizations based in Córdoba, the Middle Magdalena, the Sierra Nevada, Boyacá, Valle del Cauca and the Eastern Plains surrendered to the authorities, confessing only to the crime of illegal arms carrying, all of them protected by Decrees 2047 and 3030 of 1990 and 303 of 1991. The largest group under the command of Ariel Otero demobilized 400 of its members in Puerto Boyacá, while in Córdoba, Fidel Castaño's Muerte a Revolucionarios del Nordeste (MRN) handed over 600 rifles and some portions of land as supposed compensation to the peasants who had been dispossessed of their plots of land. Also, a redoubt of about 200 men, formerly under the command of Rodríguez Gacha, took advantage of the amnesty in Pacho (Cundinamarca). As a result, since 1992, there has been a significant reduction in the number of civilian murders attributed to the self-defense groups in previous years. In practice, however, these structures continued to be active, maintaining a low profile.

The self-defense groups in the Magdalena Medio region became embroiled in a brutal struggle with their former partners in the Medellin Cartel in 1990. Henry Perez, the first commander, had been killed by a gunman during the celebration of the feast of the Virgen del Carmen in July 1991, and Ariel Otero, his successor aligned with the Cali Cartel, would suffer the same fate in early 1992. The surviving force atomized and some of its remnants entered Escobar's service, while other gangs, such as the one headed by Ramon Isaza, withdrew from the area.

Meanwhile, in the southern part of the region, near Honda, Tolima, Jaime Eduardo Rueda Rocha, Galan's assassin, escaped from prison a year ago and now head of a gang of 150 criminals, came to the fore. Seeking to position himself as the top leader, he killed and dismembered the mayor of Puerto Boyaca in March 1992, then threw his body and those of four of his companions into the Magdalena River. But his rise was cut short by a GOES patrol that shot him and 10 members of his security force in a restaurant in Honda on April 23 of the same year. After his death, vigilante activity in the area diminished considerably, as they opted to mimic their criminal activities. With Escobar eliminated in December 1993, Ramón Isaza regained control of Magdalena Medio.

The paramilitary groups held a truce between 1992 and 1994, with the surrender of some weapons and land, and were reinvigorated at the end of the Gaviria four-year term. Thus, after Escobar's death in 1993, the Autodefensas Campesinas de Córdoba y Urabá (ACCU), under the command of Fidel Castaño and Carlos Castaño, expanded with the support of hundreds of demobilized EPL members, persecuted by the FARC-EP and the EPL dissidence led by Francisco Caraballo.

The Cathedral and Escape

On June 19, 1991, the drug lord voluntarily entered prison in exchange for not being extradited to the U.S. However, in order to do so, he demanded from the government - among other things - that he be held in an exclusive prison, arguing that he could be in danger of death if he were to be held in an ordinary correctional facility. Thus, the government authorized the construction of the site that would later become the worst shame of the Colombian prison system: called La Catedral (The Cathedral). A precinct built "to measure", which was erected on land acquired by Escobar himself, and which had innumerable luxuries for him and his associates, in addition to strong security provided by the Colombian Army outside, restricted air space and the prison authorities appointed by the state to guard his confinement, most of whom were Escobar's hitmen in prison guard uniforms.

Within almost a year of his imprisonment in early July 1992, Escobar had become a high-ranking extortionist. He stopped exporting cocaine and began collecting large sums of money from other drug traffickers. Suspicious of his closest allies Galeano and Moncada, claiming that they were hiding $20 million from him, Escobar ordered the execution of both. The subsequent purge among those closest to the two capos and their families left some 50 dead. The Government and the Prosecutor's Office, upon learning of the serious events and in order to prevent Escobar from continuing to commit crimes from his comfortable prison, ordered his transfer to a new prison. But in dark conditions that demonstrated once again the power of corruption and the fear that the dangerous drug trafficker generated after kidnapping the vice minister of Justice Eduardo Mendoza and the director of prisons of INPEC Colonel Hernando Navas, who anticipated the movements of the Government to Escobar, and at the same time it was discovered that the soldiers in charge of guarding the outskirts of the prison had been bribed by the drug lord.

Escape from the Cathedral

On July 22, 1992, Escobar, his brother Roberto and nine of his men escaped from the prison after kicking one of the back walls of the building built with plaster for this purpose. The capo and his henchmen fled walking, going around the mountains and taking advantage of the fog that covered the area and the blackout of the so-called Gaviria Hour. The escape of the capo meant the biggest mockery of the Gaviria government in the public opinion and the Colombian justice system would end up being discredited internationally.

The government, touched to its core, created the Search Bloc, a body made up of the National Police, the National Army and U.S. anti-drug forces to hunt down the fugitives and dismantle their criminal empire once and for all. The leaders of the Cali Cartel set off the war again by setting off a car bomb in Medellín that they attributed to their enemies in Antioquia.

Faced with the onslaught of the state forces, they reactivated their campaign with a series of attacks in which they executed 30 uniformed men and a judge between September and October 1992. But this time the situation had changed abruptly for the cartel: the death of Galeano and Moncada generated a fracture within the organization. Diego Murillo Bejarano "Don Berna," the security chief of the murdered capos, and the Castaño brothers, aligned themselves with the narcos of the Valle in a broad alliance against Escobar, which included corrupt officers of the Search Bloc and several of their former associates. With the information they were able to provide to the authorities, they dealt major blows to the "Patrón's" networks. On October 28, Tyson (Brances Alexander Muñoz), one of his most important military chiefs, was killed in a special operation.

Escobar tried at that time to negotiate his rededication and had authorized the surrender of several of his closest lieutenants, among them his brother Roberto, alias *"Popeye"* (John Jairo Velásquez, deceased in 2020), *"Otto" and "Mugre"*, unleashed in response a new all-out war. Dozens of gunmen executed a hundred policemen until February and car bombs reappeared in the big cities from December 1992 onwards. Although the mechanisms were no longer as sophisticated, the human and material losses were heavy, since the attacks were no longer directed at a specific target, but were totally indiscriminate. In Medellín 19 people died, in Bogotá 39 and in Barrancabermeja 16. The Aburrá Valley was affected by 3 attacks in December 1992 and in Bogotá the explosions began in January 1993: on the 20th in the north, on the 30th in front of the Chamber of Commerce, in mid-February in two commercial areas and on April 15 in the Parque de la 93.

Despite the hard onslaught of the terrorists, the authorities assassinated up to March 1993 100 assassins and 10 military chiefs of the cartel, among them *El Chopo* (Mario Castaño Molina), *HH* (Hernán Darío Henao) and *El Palomo* (Jhonny Edison Rivera), all of whom were trusted by Escobar. Also 1,900 suspected members of the organization were arrested, and 18 high-ranking members of its military wing surrendered. This, together with the defeat by rival gangs of its trigger groups, in a war that left 300 dead, ended up decisively weakening the Medellín group, which in 8 months lost 80% of its war capacity. In addition, on January 30, a paramilitary structure called *Los Pepes* (**Perseguidos** por Pablo Escobar), behind which were the Castaño brothers, made its public appearance and dedicated itself to killing the capo's front men, accountants, lawyers and relatives, as well as destroying his properties and undermining his finances.

Death

On December 2, 1993, one day after his 44th birthday, Escobar was cornered by the security forces and by the threats against his family. The drug lord tried to negotiate his surrender, conditioning it on the departure of his wife and children from the country, but this time his proposal did not find an echo among the Executive Power. Although he managed to evade the Search Bloc for six more months, the death of his security chief, *El Angelito* (León Puerta Muñoz), in October 1993, left him unprotected, now under the command of hired killers. Finally, the concern for the situation of his wife and children - refugees in Tequendama Residences under strict police surveillance after unsuccessfully seeking asylum in the United States and Germany - was used as bait by the government to lure Escobar, who up to that moment was suffering from gastric problems and had allegedly announced the formation of an armed group called *Antioquia Independiente (Independent Antioquia)*.

The Search Bloc devoted itself to the task of locating Escobar until, after a year and four months of intense intelligence work, on December 1, 1993, it succeeded in tracing and locating six calls Escobar made to his son.

Previously, DIJIN signals intelligence units had tracked down the capo's whereabouts using French and British technology acquired by the National Police in 1991 and operated by Colombian police intelligence officers and non-commissioned officers. In an interview with Gilberto Rodríguez Orejuela, he said he had helped purchase the technology.

That same afternoon of December 2, 1993, units of the search block surrounded the house where he was hiding once he was located in the Los Olivos neighborhood, a middle class neighborhood in the city of Medellín. At the time he was discovered in his hideout, he was being guarded by only one hitman, Alvaro de Jesus Agudelo (*El Limon*), who was killed when he confronted the agents who entered the house where the drug lord was hiding.

Seeing himself cornered, Pablo Escobar tried to escape through the roofs of the surrounding houses and was shot three times. The first of the three shots that hit him came from the rifle of an agent covering the rear exit of the house. He received it when he tried to retrace his steps, on the roof, and was hit in the back of the shoulder by a bullet that lodged between teeth 35 and 36, according to forensic experts. The hood would probably fall on the tile roof after this impact. A second shot, located in the left thigh, prevented him from getting up again. Finally, the third and most controversial hit his head at close range (this would later be denied by the Search Bloc) and entered from the right side of the face, near the ear, to exit on the left. The bullet killed him instantly.

There are several hypotheses about his death:

- He committed suicide by shooting himself under the ear. This version coincides with the motto of Los Extraditables: "We prefer a grave in Colombia to a prison in the United States" and is the version defended by his family.

- He was shot by a sniper from the *Los Pepes* group.

- He was shot by a DIJIN officer who was part of the Search Bloc.

- He was shot by a Delta Force (DF) sniper.

- He was shot to death by Colonel Hugo Heliodoro Aguilar, who led the assault group that arrived at the house.

- He was shot by Carlos Castaño Gil, top leader of the United Self-Defense Forces of Colombia (AUC), according to a confession by a paramilitary named José Antonio Hernández, known by the *alias* John.

- This scene is depicted in a famous painting by Botero, and is the official version.

Reactions to his death

Escobar's death generated different reactions: his family and protégés mourned his death, and his funeral was attended by thousands of people, mostly from the poor neighborhoods of Medellín. The press and the government considered it a triumph in the fight against illicit drugs and the beginning of the end of drug trafficking, which has not happened to date; today guerrillas and organized crime groups known as Bacrim (criminal gangs) dispute the drug trafficking business. Although immediately after their demise, the Cali and Norte del Valle cartels had control of drug trafficking until their respective dissolutions.

Among the myths about his death is one that says he did not die, that he hired a double and that he is in hiding enjoying his money.

His image is still very relevant today. His photos are sold next to those of Che Guevara.

His legend is part of the tourist circuit of Medellín. His hacienda in the countryside is now a museum visited by thousands of tourists a year.

Exhumation

Pablo Escobar's corpse was exhumed on October 28, 2006 at the request of some of his relatives in order to take a

DNA sample to confirm the alleged paternity of an extra-marital child and to clear any doubts about the identity of the body that had been buried next to his parents for 12 years. A video of the moment was broadcasted by RCN channel, a fact that upset his son Juan Sebastián Marroquín (Juan Pablo Escobar) who accused his uncle Roberto Escobar Gaviria and the kingpin's nephew Nicolás Escobar -who coordinated the act- of being "merchants of death".

In popular culture

As one of Colombia's and the world's most famous characters, Escobar has been portrayed in countless formats for different audiences around the world. He has been the subject of study in documentaries, and several actors have played him.

Television series

- *El Patrón del Mal (Escobar el Patrón del Mal) (*2012): Starring Hernán Mauricio Ocampo (Escobar as a child), Mauricio Mejía (Escobar as a young Escobar), and Andrés Parra (Escobar as an adult).

- *Los Tres Caínes (*2013): Starring Colombian actor Juan Pablo Franco.

- *Bloque de búsqueda (*2016): played by Arturo Álvarez.

- *Surviving Escobar, alias JJ (Surviving Escobar - Alias JJ)*: Played by Juan Pablo Franco.

- *En la boca del lobo*: Played by Fabio Restrepo.

- *Narcos* (2015 - 2017): As himself (archive): He was played by Brazilian actor Wagner Moura.

- *El Chapo* (2017 - 2018): Played by Mauricio Mejía. Netflix series

- *El General Naranjo (*2019 - 2020): Played by Colombian actor Federico Rivera.

Films

- *Blow* (2001): Starring New Zealand actor Cliff Curtis.

- *Escobar: Paradise Lost* (2014): Starring Benicio del Toro

- *American Made* (2017): Interpreted by Mauricio Mejía.

- *Loving Pablo* (2017): He was played by Spanish actor and director Javier Bardem.

Documentaries

- *The private archives of Pablo Escobar*

- *Pablo Escobar, angel or demon?*

- The television channel ESPN made a documentary in 2010 on Monday, June 21 about the life of soccer player Andres Escobar Saldarriaga and drug trafficker Pablo Emilio Escobar Gaviria and described through testimonies the links between Colombian professional soccer teams and drug traffickers from the Medellin and Cali cartels in the late 1970s and the 1980s and 1990s.

- In 2012 Caracol Televisión Colombia made a documentary called Los Tiempos de Pablo Escobar Lecciones de una Época.

Music

Several songs of different musical genres have been composed in honor of Pablo Escobar and others in which he is mentioned.

Other books by United Library

https://campsite.bio/unitedlibrary

Milton Keynes UK
Ingram Content Group UK Ltd.
UKHW050839150224
437886UK00015B/357